Old KEITH

by
Alan Cooper

When Rothiemay Hall burned down in January 1916 (see inside the back cover), Peter Tewnion of Rothiemay discovered the fire and raised the alarm.

© Alan Cooper 1999
First published in the United Kingdom, 1999,
by Stenlake Publishing, Ochiltree Sawmill, The Lade,
Ochiltree, Ayrshire, KA18 2NX
Telephone / Fax: 01290 423114

ISBN 1 84033 086 4

FURTHER READING

The books listed below were used by the author during his research. None of them are available from Stenlake Publishing. Those interested in finding out more are advised to contact their local bookshop or reference library.

Archibald, Rev. J., *History of the Episcopal Church of Keith*, 1890.
Barclay, W., *The Schools and Schoolmasters of Banffshire*, 1925.
Collins, Thomas, *A Martyr in Scotland, The Life & Times of John Ogilvie*, 1955.
Cowie, J. W., *Recollections of Keith*, 1928.
Cramond, William, *The Church of Keith*, 1890.
Ettles, B. & Shanks, I., *Manuscript to Microchip, A History of Keith Schools*, 1998.
Gordon, Rev. J. F. S., *The Book of the Chronicles of Keith*, 1880.
Macfarlane, W. H., *Twixt the Land and the Moss*, 1922.
Welsh, G. C., *Keith and its Lairds*, 1958.
Banffshire Herald, 1893 onwards.

A fragment is all that remains of Keith's oldest building, the sixteenth century Tower of Milton. The building was ruinous by 1742, following which most of it was removed. It was often the case that stones from disused buildings were carted off to be used elsewhere, and this may have been what happened to the Tower of Milton. The castle originally lay in the lands of Drumnakeith, an estate which was mentioned as 'the lands of Drumbeth or Drumkeyth' in a grant of land in the fourteenth century. In the late fifteenth century the estate's owners, James Ogilvie and his wife Agnes Gordon, divided the lands creating the estates of Milton and Kempcairn. It was through this division that their son, George Ogilvie, became the first Laird of Milton.

INTRODUCTION

The town of Keith developed in three distinctive phases, the first of which was the settlement down by the River Isla, centred around the church and churchyard. Modern-day Keith dates from 1750 when the Earl of Findlater and Seafield laid out a new planned town with a square and three parallel streets – Moss Street, Mid Street and Land Street. The third phase of development began in 1817 on the other side of the river when the Earl Fife established the village of Fife-Keith. This was originally to have been called Waterloo but the name was never used. The three parts were united as the police burgh of Keith in 1889.

The lands of Keith originally belonged to the Abbey of Kinloss, and had been granted to them by a charter, circa 1195, in the reign of King William the Lion. 'Geth', as it was called in the charter, was then part of the Barony of Strathisla which extended from the Balloch to the Knock and included Grange where the monks had a residence, the Tower of Strathisla.

A fragment of the original church, which was taken down in 1819 and replaced by a new church nearby, is still visible in the churchyard. The people of Keith not only witnessed, but sometimes took part in important events around the church, as in 1700 when they seized the celebrated freebooter James Macpherson. He was hanged in Banff afterwards, and is reputed to have played a rant he had composed in the prison entitled 'Macpherson's Farewell', before breaking his fiddle on his knee and throwing the pieces into the grave prepared for him.

A gang of raiders, led by Peter Roy McGregor, were captured in Keith in 1667. Their activities were well documented at their trial in Edinburgh, where the charges against them included robbery and murder. It was stated that 'with a number of 40 men [they] did assault the town of Keith for not paying black mail, and fought against those who opposed them, in particular against Alexander Gordon of Glengaroch, and his brother Thomas Gordon and John Ogilvie of Milton and their followers, and did wound and mutilate the said John Ogilvie and Thomas Gordon, and the pannells themselves being ill wounded at the time and not able to flee far, were taken prisoners the next day and conveyed to the tolbooth of Edinburgh'. McGregor and another of the gang were sentenced to be taken to the Market Cross in Edinburgh, where their right hands were cut off before they were hanged, following which their bodies were chained up on public display as a warning to others. The executioner made such a mess of cutting off their right hands, requiring many cuts with the knife to do the job, that he was dismissed from his post.

In 1650 the Marquis of Montrose, the captured general of King Charles's army in Scotland, arrived in Keith on his way to Edinburgh and his inevitable execution there. A halt was called in the town. He was described as being bare-headed, wearing a suit of decayed tartan, and mounted on a miserable Highland pony with his feet bound together by a rope passing under the animal's belly. It happened to be a Sunday and Montrose was compelled to listen to a tirade in the churchyard at Keith from the parish minister. The preacher's sermon from the Old Testament was directed at Montrose & included the words 'as thy sword hath made women childless so shall thy mother be childless among women'. Montrose maintained his dignity, however, and merely remarked 'rail on sir, I am bound to listen to you'.

There are some interesting references in the church records relating to Keith and the Jacobite rebellion of 1715. On 25 September that year it was recorded that 'this day the Earl of Huntly began his march to the rebel's army with his cavalcade of horse, the foot being to march to Merins. This day, immediately after sermon, the writer Mr John Skinner, was seized by a party of Auchynachie's men as was pretended by the Earl of Huntly's order, and very harshly dealt with and the school much broke, etc.' Another entry, following the battle of Sherriffmuir, reads: '18th December 1715. This day the Earl of Huntly passed through Keith on his return, very disheartened like'. The Earl – or more correctly the Marquis of Huntly – was returning to his father's residence at Gordon Castle, Fochabers. Soon afterwards it was recorded that 'about sixty or more of the Strathdone rebels headed by Black Joke, alias John Forbes, and Sclater Forbes, came and lay in the town about a week, where they committed unheard of insolencies, robbed the school chamber and carried off many things, as did afterwards about the beginning of the year Glenbucket's men who were also monsters of wickedness'.

In 1746 the army of the Catholic Young Pretender, Prince Charles Edward Stuart, was retreating towards Inverness, pursued by Government forces led by the Duke of Cumberland. The armies would eventually meet at Culloden Moor. However, on 20 March 1746, when Cumberland was still in Aberdeen, an advance party of his men comprised of 70 Argyllshire Militia and 30 Kingaton's Horse under Captain Campbell were spending the night in the church in Keith. They were surrounded and heavily defeated by a party of Jacobites from Fochabers, commanded by a Frenchman, major Nicholas Glascoe. After more than half-an-hour of fighting some of the Government soldiers lay dead, but most were captured, with only six managing to escape, one of them getting away on foot after his horse fell into a bog in the darkness.

These events are some of the many that feature in Keith's varied history, and the pictures and text that follow aim to provide an insight into some other aspects of the town's past.

The original town of Keith was situated by the River Isla and centred around the church and churchyard; the school was adjacent to the church. Important events such as court cases were held in the church. Writing in 1880, Rev. Gordon described old Keith as having been made up of a hamlet at Begg's Brae built on the glebe, and a narrow and filthy High Street with access for wheelbarrows only. He stated that it had been swept away during the nineteenth century. According to a different source there had once been a row of houses between the new and old bridges, separated from the river by small gardens. Very little trace of old Keith remains today, though a fragment of the church can be seen in the graveyard, and five blind arches, or kreams (now bricked up), which stand in the south-west corner of the churchyard dyke, were originally used by merchants at the Summer Eve's Fair.

Auld Brig Keith.

M. 404.

One of the legends concerning the Auld Brig asserts that it was built after a couple's son drowned while trying to cross the Isla. The bridge bears a stone with the date 1609 and the names Thomas Murray and Janet Lindsay, set on the south side above the arch, though there are no known references to these people locally. Daniel Defoe, author of *Robinson Crusoe*, came this way in 1706 during his tour of Britain and described the bridge as 'exceedingly high and steep'. At one time the date-stone fell or was thrown into the river, but was apparently reinstated when the bridge was repaired in 1822.

The Central Banffshire Auction Mart Company Ltd. opened their premises at Keith on Saturday 26 September 1903, beginning with a sale of pigs at 11.30 a.m., and then continued with sales of fat cattle and store cattle. 'Mr Gordon Rhind, Mid Street, was the first purchaser – of a pair of fat pigs from Mr McGlashan of the Royal Hotel for £6 – and he had a cordial cheer' (*Banffshire Herald*, 3 October 1903). The new mart company in Keith was a public company, owned by its shareholders, many of them local farmers, and with capital of £3,000. The premises were bought for £2,000 from the previous owners and £700-£800 spent on improvements. 'During intervals spread over a period of nearly twenty years more or less successful sales were conducted in the town. . . . During the last seven or eight years no sales were held, and while one of the marts had been converted into dwelling-houses, etc, that at Old Keith stood little changed, and was used for killing shops, etc. (*Banffshire Herald*, 3 October 1903).

In the eighteenth century the stagecoach replaced the post-horse system of mail delivery and resulted in the need for better bridges and roads. Union Bridge was built in 1770 and was originally only 16 feet wide, but was widened by another 9 feet in 1816. The bridge was widened again in 1912 when very distinctive new parapets (above) were built. According to the council, improvements were needed due to the increase in traffic using the bridge, and the surveys they conducted make interesting reading. During one week in February 1912 the average number of motor vehicles using the bridge per day was 18; the average number of horse-drawn vehicles was 192; and the average number of horses, cattle, etc., crossing the bridge was 389. These figures were an increase on the traffic in September 1911 when the numbers for the same three categories were 38, 147, and 226 respectively (*Banffshire Herald*, 11 May 1912).

Keith Town station. The Great North of Scotland Railway line from Huntly to Keith was opened to passenger traffic in 1856. The line from Keith Junction to Elgin was completed by the Highland Railway, opening on 18 August 1858. The station in the picture (originally called Earlsmill) was opened on 20 April 1896 but in 1897 was renamed Keith Town. The previous station, also called Earlsmill and dating from 1862, had been about fifty yards further along the line towards the mill that it took its name from. Friction between the GNSR and Highland Railway meant that the GNSR sometimes refused to stop its trains at Keith Junction, with the result that passengers who were travelling further west with the Highland Railway were forced to walk from Keith Town to get their connection at Keith Junction.

Earlsmill takes its name from the Earl of Findlater & Seafield who became the owner of Keith in 1704 when the previous owners, Mary Ogilvie and her husband Lord Oliphant, heavily in debt, were forced to sell the Milton Estate. It appears that this wasn't sufficient for them to pay off their creditors, as the title to the lands was not cleared until 1727 when the Earl of Findlater & Seafield paid William Duff of Braco, Grange, money due on bonds granted by the Oliphants. Earlsmill had a long history of milling in various forms. At one time there was a waulk mill, dyeworks, and a snuff mill, and in 1880 there was a threshing mill. A fire in 1925 destroyed the oatmeal mill but it was rebuilt and new machinery installed. Today the area is completely bare, with nothing to indicate that people ever lived or earned their living there.

THE LINN, KEITH. B.5340.

The Linn is a beautiful feature of Keith, but with the waters of the Isla crashing down onto the rocks below the waterfall this spot is also sometimes quite noisy. The mill on the right was called Mills of Keith, and in 1957 was purchased by the owners of Strathisla Distillery (called Milton Distillery until 1951) and turned into a new distillery called Glenkeith. An overhead pipeline was installed for the conveyance of malt between the two distilleries. Milton Distillery was founded in 1786.

The Isla Bank Mills were run by the Kynoch family from 1805 when George Kynoch bought the flax mill and bleachgreen and started a firm called Kynoch & Christie. To begin with it was a small-scale enterprise, but in the late nineteenth century new buildings were erected right over the old mill, which was left intact and in working order until the new buildings were ready. In 1954, G. & G. Kynoch floated on the stock exchange. The company prospered, winning recognition for its contribution to exports with the Queen's Award to Industry in 1966. It was the first Scottish woollen manufacturer to receive the award, and honours went to its executives – a CBE to Gordon Kynoch and an OBE to Edgar Winter. With a trend towards lighter clothes, however, and a move away from traditional sports jackets, suits and flannels, the business went into decline in the following decades. Eventually the mills were closed and the buildings are now used by other industries.

In 1916 it was reported that nine of the 53 mill workers at Isla Bank who had joined up to fight in the war had been killed. While the mill owners had difficulty in running the business because of a shortage of labour, there were a great many orders to deal with. In 1916 orders from the Government alone included 10,000 army blankets, 400,000 yards of grey flannel, 35,000 yards of khaki flannel, and 35,000 yards of Black Watch tartan. As well as the woollen mill, there was a fertiliser business (sold in 1923) at Isla Bank. In 1915 a worker, John Moggach, died from anthrax, a disease he had become infected with during his work, which involved mixing and bagging fertiliser made from crushed bones, horn, hair, etc. His widowed mother sued the company over the loss of her son as she was dependant upon him, but lost her case as she had failed to inform them of his death until after his funeral (i.e. not quickly enough), although it was accepted by all concerned in the case that her son had died of anthrax contracted whilst at work.

GRAMMAR SCHOOL, KEITH

Keith Grammar School in Church Road was built in 1833 opposite the parish church, and remained in use until 1965 when a new grammar school was opened. Originally the school consisted solely of two large classrooms for the 200 pupils, one used by the headmaster, James Smith, and the other by his assistant, Mr Stewart. When the school first opened pupils had to pay fees, with the result that many had very little formal education. It was quite common for children to attend school during the winter months then work at other times – the usual occupation was the herding of cattle, an important task before fields were fenced. The original 1833 school was a single-storey building, but was steadily expanded, most notably in the 1880s and in 1908.

Keith Grammar School.

The earliest school in Keith was the Edindaich Mortifiers School, which was situated in the churchyard adjacent to the church. The land for the school was gifted by Alexander Ogilvie, a lawyer in Edinburgh. One of the early teachers was John Skinner who was also a session clerk at the church and who wrote about the abuse he suffered at the hands of the rebel soldiers as they passed through the town in 1715. In 1819 the church and school were both taken down, with the school moving to the upper part of the town's jail at the bottom of the square, entry to which was by a stone stair from the outside. The jail was used as a school until 1833.

The new parish church was opened by the minister, Rev. James McLean, on 14 March 1819 in the presence of a large congregation. It had seating for 1,800 and a tower 120 feet high. At the time it was simply called the parish church, and the name St Rufus was not adopted until 1929. The old church had been situated in the graveyard, and was taken down in 1819 along with the adjacent school.

The restoration of the monarchy in 1660 led to the re-establishment of the Episcopal church, but the succession of William III in 1688 brought this period to an end. The minister in Keith at the time, Rev. Sir James Strachan, was deposed for refusing to pray for the new king and queen, but continued to preach in the meeting-house at Allanbuie. During the 1715 rebellion, as the Jacobite supporters came through Keith on their way south, they installed Rev. James Sibbald of Allanbuie in the parish church, but he left the area when the rebellion collapsed. Attempts were made to stamp out the Episcopal church, with meetings restricted to nine members (plus the members of the household) from 1719, and reduced to five after 1746. Those who came to hear a popular preacher risked imprisonment or banishment to the colonies. A man was sent to prison along with the witnesses to the ceremony for having his child baptised by the Rev. Sibbald at a house near Birkenburn. A meeting-house at Rosarie was in use before the '45 and was probably burned by Cumberland's men. The first proper Episcopal church was built in Mid Street in 1807, and replaced by the Holy Trinity Church in Seafield Avenue in 1882.

The main ceremony for the formal opening of the war memorials on 11 November 1923 was held in the parish church, with only the actual unveiling and dedication taking place outside. The *Banffshire Herald* gave a very detailed account of the event: 'Boy scouts and girl guides took up a position in front of the memorials, the Gordons took up a position on the left of the memorials, while the pipers went inside the enclosure. At the corners of the two memorials were Gordons, standing with arms reversed. The Duke [of Richmond] stepped forward and pronounced the dedicatory and thanksgiving prayer, which was followed by the lament 'The Flowers of the Forest' by the Battalion pipers. The 'Last Post' was then sounded.' The Duke and others laid wreathes and the ceremony concluded with the singing of the national anthem, the benediction by Rev. Matthew Stewart and the sounding of the reveille.

The Turner Hospital was opened in 1880 and named after the late Dr Robert Turner. Rev. Gordon, writing at the time, described it as standing 'at the top of Begg's Brae, where formerly there was a hattrel of poor cots belonging to the glebe' (Gordon, p270). The hospital cost £1,216 to build and had 8 beds with a staff of two – a matron and a probationer. The number of beds was soon increased to 12 and then 16. Following his narrow escape in a railway accident at Thirsk, George Kynoch gave money to the hospital, and a wing with 8 beds called the Kynoch Wards was opened in 1895. By 1923 there were plans to raise £2,000-£3,000 for an operating theatre and other facilities.

The Longmore Hall was built in 1872 at a cost of £2,000 and was presented to the town by William Longmore, a local businessman. The opening ceremony was held on 24 January 1873 with about 600 attending the event. Though not a native of the parish, Longmore told the audience that he had spent the best of his days at Keith and owed much of his prosperity to the area. A great variety of entertainments were held in the hall, including concerts and amateur dramatics. Some famous names appeared there including Dr Walford Bodie, at one time the second highest paid entertainer in Scotland after Harry Lauder. Bodie visited in February and October

The Longmore Hall, Keith

1910 with his show of magic, electrical powers and hypnotism. His beautiful assistant, La Belle Electra, also came to Keith with him. Bodie could use his powers to make her light, allowing her to float unsupported, or else heavy, when she could resist the efforts of six men to lift her. Bodie's eldest son also appeared in the show as a conjuror and illusionist. Before the opening of Keith's first cinema in 1915, there were occasional cinematic shows in the Longmore Hall. One regular visitor was Walker & Company's Cinematograph from Aberdeen, which made its first visit to Keith on 10 December 1896, and presented the first cinematic performance the town had seen. In April 1900 the company showed Boer War pictures in the Longmore Hall. Some of the silent films were accompanied by pipers and drummers, and in their 1903 show the company presented the famous violinist J. Scott Skinner, the 'Strathspey King'.

The fine block of buildings on the right, known as the Royal Hotel Buildings, were built in 1883 and included shops, a house, and stables as well as the hotel. The original owner was James Walker, watchmaker and jeweller, who had a shop on the ground floor and rented out the buildings before selling them (along with other property) in 1898 to Alexander Harper, tenant of the Royal Hotel at the time. Harper sold out in 1901 to Mr McGlashan of the Saltoun Arms Hotel, Fraserburgh. The church on the left, originally the Free Church, was opened on 28 December 1845. The driving force behind the church was Rev. Archibald McGilvray, a native of Greenock, who was minister from 1843 until his death in 1869. A manse was also built, as well as a Free Church school next to the church. When Rev. McGilvray first came to Keith he rented rooms in Mid Street above the offices of G. & G. Kynoch.

THE BOWLING GREEN, KEITH.

B.5339.

In 1878 William Longmore decided to purchase the land adjacent to Longmore Hall to make a bowling green for the use of the town, and on 17 June the following year the bowling club was opened. Longmore was the owner of the Milton Distillery (renamed Strathisla Distillery in 1951) which became a public company in 1880 called William Longmore and Company, with the sale of 7,000 shares at £5 each. Longmore, also a banker and merchant, had bought the distillery in 1830. He died in 1882. The club initially had 30 members, but by 1909 the roll exceeded 100 names. Women were admitted as members in 1928.

Junior Department, Keith Grammar School.

In 1863 subscriptions were collected for the purpose of building a girls' school, and a committee was appointed to oversee the project. A site was selected and half an acre of land purchased from the Earl of Seafield, for which an annual feu-duty of £2 was paid. The school cost £435 to build, and was opened on 20 November 1865. It was named Green's Female Infant School in consideration of a gift from the widow of the late Robert Green, banker in Keith. The first teachers appointed were Mrs Taylor and her daughter, Miss Jane Taylor, who had been running a similar school for a number of years in Keith. They received all the fees from the pupils. In 1924 most of the school was demolished; the only parts retained were the wing on the west and the assembly hall behind it.

Moss Street. At the opening of the replacement to Green's School in August 1925, Canon Macdonald criticised the committee that had been responsible for the old building. He observed that: 'Externally it was a beautiful school. Very few schools in the country had such a facade, such a nice appearance. Yet for all that the school was a death trap for the little children. There was scarcely a room in the school into which a ray of God's bright sunshine entered from one year's end to another. There was no ventilation.' (*Banffshire Herald*, 29 August 1925). By comparison the new school was described as 'perhaps not a gem of architectural beauty from the outside', but 'the one-time cold and cheerless class rooms are gone . . . the aim of having the interior as bright and as wholesome as possible has been accomplished . . . the class rooms are lit by large windows which permit of plenty fresh air. The building is heated by central heating.'

The Playhouse, Keith's second cinema, was opened by Provost Thomson on 29 July 1935. The building was completed in ten weeks from the laying of the first stone, and the architect was Major Cattanach of Kingussie. It had seating for 700, with 200 in the balcony, and was decorated chiefly in green and brown. According to reports in the press it was the first in the north of Scotland to have 'the new wide range Western Electric equipment, which gives a wonderful range of sound' (*Banffshire Herald*, 27 July 1935). At the opening ceremony the public, admitted free of charge, filled the stalls area, while the balcony was reserved for the town council and shareholders in the company. In the first week the main film was *The Gay Divorce* starring Fred Astaire and Ginger Rogers. The cinema showed its last film in June 1982, and the building continued to be used for bingo until September. In 1986 it was sold and turned into a furniture store.

Drum Road dates from the 1890s. At that time people in Keith were still being wakened in the mornings by the town drummer or bellman. George Beadie used a bell during his rounds, and was succeeded by John Anderson who used bagpipes and a drum. John Crosby, popularly known as 'Johnny Coskie', usually went round the town at 5 a.m. and 8 p.m., using a drum in dry weather and a bugle when it was wet. At new year he made door to door calls to collect contributions from the households he wakened. He died in 1877 and was succeeded by Walter 'Wattie' Scott who went round the streets with a bell and also acted as town crier. When told that his bell was cracked, he replied 'it's nae meesic I'm pey'd to gie, it's informashun'. (*Banffshire Herald*, 17 January 1903). He gave up the job in 1898 and died in 1903.

In the photograph the sign reads:

77.M.M.
GERMAN FIELD GUN
CAPTURED BY
6TH BATT. GOR. HRS.
AT LOOS
ON 25TH SEPT. 1915.

His Grace
The Duke of Richmond and Gordon, K.G
Unveiling Gun at Keith 15th Dec.1915.

In November 1915 this captured gun was on display in London at Horse Guards Parade. The idea to bring it to Keith, the headquarters of the 6th Battn. Gordon Highlanders, was apparently the Duke of Richmond's, as he explained at the unveiling ceremony: 'it occurred to me that for recruiting purposes a visit from one of our captives would not be out of place (cheers), and I can tell you even more than that! I have a communication from the Military Secretary of the Scottish Command saying that later on one of these guns is to find a permanent home in Keith. . . . We are here today and gone tomorrow but that gun, which is going eventually to find its permanent home at Keith, will be a record for all time to future generations of the gallantry of the Gordon Highlanders.' (*Banffshire Herald*, 18 December 1915). The gun was exhibited at the drill hall for three days then moved to Banff and other towns.

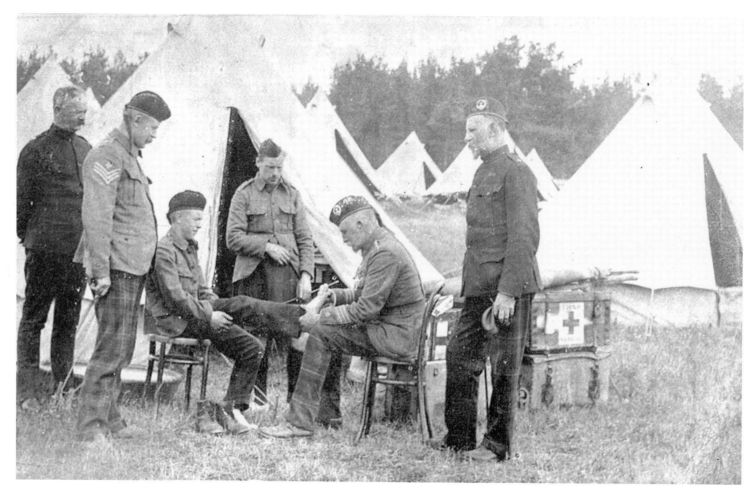

In 1909 the annual camp of the Gordon Highlanders Territorials was held on a moor at Braewynner, Enzie, with about 2,300 attending. The camp lasted for two weeks, although many could not get leave from their employers to attend the second week. In addition to the exercises during the week, the camp was an event in itself, attracting many visitors, especially on the Sundays when the part-time soldiers were allowed to entertain their friends. Thousands came by all kinds of transport (many of them by bicycle), with large crowds from Keith, Fochabers, Huntly and Aberdeen. Among the tents was a YMCA tent with a piano, gramophone, writing materials and magazines, and during the week concerts were held there. This postcard, franked 20 July 1909, was sent to a Miss Tough in Elgin with the message 'Will you be at the Glen Games? J. S. B. Coy, 6th Batt. Gordon Highlanders, Camp Keith'.

Keith Boy Scouts

Sent in June 1919, this postcard shows the Keith scouts with their scoutmaster, Miss Kynoch-Shand, who took over the running of the troop in 1916 when the previous scoutmaster went off to fight in the war. Scouting had begun in Keith in 1909 under the guidance of A. D. Craigmyle of the grammar school, and scouts took part in the proclamation procession on Tuesday 10 May 1910, when George V was proclaimed king by Provost Cameron from a specially erected platform in the middle of Reidhaven Square. This was the first such event in Keith, as previously only royal burghs had been allowed to perform the ceremony. The procession to the square left the Institute at 7.50 p.m., headed by the police, and followed by the town's postmen, territorials, scouts, magistrates and other officials. 'Following the territorials came perhaps the most interesting body of all, namely the Boy Scouts. . . . The boys in their khaki blouses and shorts made a remarkably smart display and attracted much attention.' (*Banffshire Herald*, 14 May 1910).

Keith Cattle Show.

RELIABLE series. 1372

Central Banffshire Farmers' Club was formed in 1872, and it held the first Keith Show on Friday 23 August of the same year, on what was then called the Market Green. The number of entries were: 96 cattle; 100 horses; 10 swine; 12 sheep; 50 poultry; 57 entries for dairy produce 57; and 17 for implements. There was a large attendance of spectators, and over £50 was taken in attendance money. During the day Keith Brass Band, under the leadership of William Smith entertained the crowds. Another great event to be held in Keith was the Summarius Fair, or Summer Eve's Fair, at one time in the eighteenth century the largest fair of its kind in Scotland. Merchants came to it from all over Scotland, to buy and sell their goods. Shops in Aberdeen were closed during the week-long event, as the owners transported all their goods to Keith on horseback. Many came from the Highlands, bringing thousands of horses and black cattle to sell. The fair was still a big event in 1880 for the sale of horses and cattle, but when it was held in September 1908 it was a horse fair, though very few horses were sold.

In 1760 thirty Catholics attended the small chapel of Auchanacie, and in 1785 the chapel of Kempcairn was built with Father William Reid as the priest. Following his death in 1825 Father Walter Lovi became the priest. It was through the efforts of Father Lovi that St Thomas's Church (right) was built. He travelled around Britain and Europe collecting donations, including an alterpiece entitled 'The Incredulity of St Thomas' by Francois Dubois, which was commissioned by King Charles X of France. The church opened on 7 August 1831. Renovation work in the years 1915-16, costing £3,000, lasted seventeen months, and it was during this period that the

copper dome was added to the church. The martyr John Ogilvie, hanged in Glasgow in 1615, was a notable Catholic from Keith. Beatified in 1929 and canonised in 1976, Ogilvie was born a Protestant in 1579, the son of Walter Ogilvie of Drum. After studying on the continent he became a Jesuit priest and returned to Scotland as a missionary, but was taken prisoner and tried for treason, his crime being to say mass. Ogilvie maintained that the Pope was head of the Church and refused to accept the authority of the king in spiritual matters. He also refused to give the names of his associates, and gained some fame for his able defence and apparent indifference to his own fate. To break down his resistance he was kept awake for eight days and nine nights by being jabbed with daggers and pins. Following that he was lifted up and dropped onto the floor of his prison. King James VI was kept informed of the case and gave orders that the priest should be executed if he failed to recant, and thus his eventual trial and sentence were formalities.

Chapel Street. The building on the right was originally the United Presbyterian Church. The site was bought for £115 in 1851, the foundation stone was laid on 22 July 1852, and the first service was held in October 1853. From 1900 it became the South United Free Church, and afterwards Keith South Church. In 1925 the church was closed and in February 1926 it was announced in the press that it was to be sold. The buyer was a builder, Thomas Robertson, who demolished it and used the stone to built some houses, including a villa for himself at the top of Broom Hill, known locally as Robertson Row. The manse in Land Street became a hotel called Mansefield Hotel.

The bar of the Gordon Arms Hotel is on the left of this picture of Mid Street. The hotel was established in 1751 and is believed to have been reconstructed or rebuilt by the Earl of Seafield in 1823. It had a large hall which was used for sittings of the Sheriff Court in 1830. Royal Mail coaches stopped daily outside the hotel. Ogilvie is a prominent name in Keith's early history, and it was a member of that family, the Second Earl of Seafield, who laid out the new town in 1750 with a market place, Reidhaven Square, and a main street, Mid Street. Moss Street and Land Street were added soon afterwards. This was a big step forward in the development of Keith, but there were those who complained about the Friday markets being moved to the new town.

Peter Annand founded his business in 1837 with a shop on Mid Street at the corner of the square. The shop subsequently moved to 99 Mid Street, then to nos. 102-104 in 1880. James Annand expanded the ironmongers by building larger premises and adding a tinsmiths and a plumbing business, acquiring the redundant Episcopal Chapel as a store.

Right: In 1894 the premises at 176-180 Mid Street were bought by William Smith, grocer, of Turriff, and his shop at number 180 opened soon afterwards. On 20 September 1915 Keith's first cinema, the Picture Palace, opened across the road at no. 167. It belonged to the Elite Syndicate, which had already opened cinemas in Buckie, Nairn and Huntly. There were two showings of *Neptune's Daughter* starring Annetta Kellerman on the first night, and later in the first week a Charlie Chaplin film, *Charlie's Night Out*, was shown. For twenty years this was the only cinema in Keith, but in 1935 the Playhouse opened. Two years later its owners, Caledonian Associated Cinemas, purchased the Picture Palace, closing it on 16 July 1938, and thereby eliminating the competition.

A gas company was formed in Keith in 1839, and building of the gasworks commenced in 1840 at a site just off Church Road. By 1843 gas street lights had been erected in Mid Street up to the square, and the service was gradually extended to the whole of the town and Fife-Keith. To begin with the cost of the gas for street lighting was met by public contributions. This system was unsatisfactory, and William Longmore paid the entire cost himself one winter. During the nineteenth century the price of gas was reduced from 16/- per 1,000 cubic feet to 6/8 for the same quantity in 1892. The amount of gas used rose to almost four million cubic feet in 1892 from 650,000 cubic feet thirty years earlier. George Kynoch of Isla Bank produced gas at his premises in Mid Street slightly earlier than the gas company, and had gas burning in his window in 1841. Large crowds assembled in the evenings to admire the latest invention and marvel at the beauty and brightness of the light.

All goods supplied here are better than the best.

135 WILLIAM BREMNER

William Bremner was one of eighteen children born to his father of the same name by three wives. A native of Keith, William Bremner Senior died in 1916 when in his 95th year. His other sons included James, a tailor in Aberdeen; Alexander, a Baptist minister in Port Glasgow; John, beadle at Chapel of Garioch church; and Thomas and Robert, both of whom were in the army. (*Banffshire Herald*, 18 November 1916).

Mid Street, Keith

The Institute Company was formed in 1884 with £2,500 of capital in 5,000 shares and consisted of many local societies, all of whom had the aim of improving people's intellectual, artistic, spiritual or scientific outlook. These societies included the Field Club, Total Abstinence Society, Philharmonic Society, Library and Reading Rooms Society, and the Keith Parish Church Young Men's Guild. The Institute itself was opened on 10 October 1886 and included a reading room and library, billiard room, lecture room and cafe. A small museum was added in August 1887. A fire the following year destroyed the library and museum and their contents, although the Institute was rebuilt in 1889 when the clock tower was added. The Institute Company only showed a profit nine times during the first forty years of its existence. In 1925, when the company was in danger of going into liquidation, the Institute was offered to the town council, an offer which was accepted.

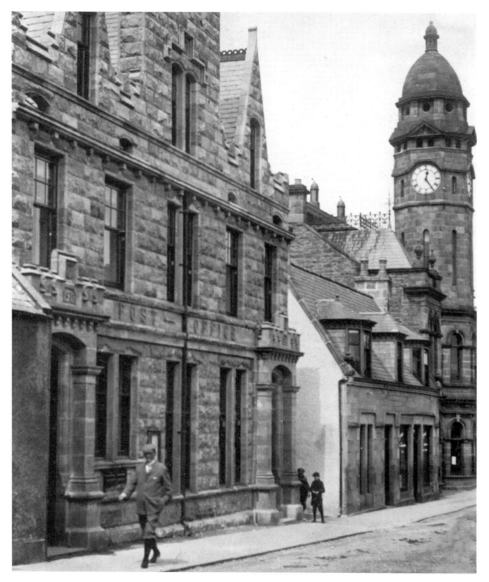

Right: The post office at 130-132 Mid Street was opened in 1912 and like the Institute was designed by F. D. Robertson, architect, of Elgin. It was built to cope with an increase in business; according to a contemporary report the recent introduction of the Old Age Pensions Act had led to an increase of 6,800 transactions per year. There was also a general increase in the amount of mail being posted. In 1895 the figures per week were: 10,500 letters, 1,000 postcards and 275 parcels. By 1911 the numbers had increased to 17,500 letters, 3,000 postcards and 670 parcels.

William Duff, first Earl Fife, founded the settlement of Newmill in an attempt to rival the Earl of Seafield's new town of Keith, begun in 1750. Newmill was never a commercial success, however, and the village contained mainly poor people and a few weavers. At Glen of Newmill there was a famous colony of Gaelic-speaking Highlanders who supported themselves largely by begging. One writer, J. W. Cowie, described how at the end of the week, after their wanderings round the parish, they gathered at Elspet Taylor's bakery where they were served with little round loaves called Beggar Baps. In 1817, the second Earl Fife founded Fife-Keith (above) as another rival to 'new' Keith, but this village also proved to be less successful than its neighbour on the other side of the Isla.

Prince Charlie's Brig, Keith.

In 1676 the 4th Marquis of Huntly (afterwards 1st Duke of Gordon) married Lady Elizabeth Howard, daughter of the Duke of Norfolk, and was on his way north to Gordon Castle, Fochabers, with his bride when he was delayed by a flood on the Burn of Aultmore. It was following this episode that the Brig of Brigend was built. (It is also referred to as Prince Charlie's Brig, though there is no known association with the prince.) In the late eighteenth century many bridges were built in the Keith area. One was constructed on the road to Newmill following a petition to the church for a collection to be made for that purpose by tenants in Newmill, Glengerrack and Montgrew. They complained that they were sometimes prevented from attending the church in Keith by the lack of a bridge. In 1772, the kirk session gave five shillings towards a bridge over the Burn of Haughs, and in 1774 nearly £2 was collected for the North Water bridge.

Main Street, Newmill. James Gordon Bennett, founder of *The New York Herald*, was born in 1795 in the parish of Enzie, the son of a poor crofter. While in his infancy the family moved to the small village of Newmill. After the death of his father, he moved with his mother and two sisters to Keith. He was educated at schools in Newmill and Keith where he became proficient in Latin and Greek. On leaving school, he worked in Keith for a haberdasher, Robert Stronach. 'Here he remained some time, and is still remembered as having been slender of build, and about six feet in height' (Gordon, p328). After Stronach became bankrupt, Bennett and his uncle, Cosmo Reid, went to Aberdeen and went into business. A few years later, however, Bennett decided to leave the country and arrived in Halifax, Nova Scotia, in May 1819, accompanied by a friend from Keith, James Wilson. He founded *The New York Herald* in 1835. It was his son, also called James Gordon Bennett, who sent Henry Morton Stanley to Africa to find David Livingstone.

The old wool mill, known locally as Shottie Hunter's. At one time flax (lint), the fibres of which were made into linen, was an important crop in the area. Every farmer grew a quantity of flax, which was pulled up by the roots and steeped in water for about six days following harvesting. After that it went through the beating mills (there were several of these in Keith), where the useful fibres were separated from the rest of the plant. These fibres then went to the heckling shed where they were prepared for spinning, which was done locally in weavers' homes. To whiten the product it was exposed to the sun in bleaching fields. There was once a great number of weavers in Keith, but following the introduction of cotton the flax industry went into rapid decline, and the weavers found themselves redundant.

40

Braehead, Keith. Until the introduction of the Distillery Act of 1824, the illicit distilling and smuggling of whisky was virtually an industry in itself, carried on by a great many farmers and crofters in the Keith area. During the years 1790 to 1803, 700 people were fined for offences related to distilling and smuggling, with 270 of them from the parish of Grange and the rest from Keith, Botriphnie, Mortlach, Boharm, and Cairnie. In 1790 John Taylor from New Keith was charged with refusing to produce the key to his flax mill. Sometimes people were caught in the act of making whisky; alternatively items used for distilling were discovered where they had been hidden – for instance under a bed, in a peat-moss, or even under a heap of dung. Prior to the Act of 1824 most of the malt whisky produced in the north of Scotland was being made illegally. The slow distilling process used by the bootleggers produced a smoother whisky than that made by the quicker technique of the licensed distilleries, which were charged duty on the length of time the process took, as well as on their output. The Distillery Act brought great changes to the industry, with massive fines of £100 introduced to deter illicit distilling and smuggling. This led to the opening of many new licensed distilleries.

Rothiemay became a burgh of barony in the thirteenth century. At one time the estate, including the village and burgh, was owned by the Earl of Atholl, but he forfeited it on his conviction for treason and in 1345 it was granted by King David II to William de Abernethy. He held the lands on the unusual condition that, if required, he should render a pair of gilt spurs to the king at Rothiemay at Whitsuntide or on the May Festival. At the height of their prosperity the Abernethy family owned lands in the counties of Banff, Berwick, Fife, Forfar, Midlothian and Stirling. Their principal residence was Rothiemay House (above), sometimes called Rothiemay Castle. Mary, Queen of Scots spent a night in the house in 1562 during her progress north to Inverness. The Abernethy family sold Rothiemay in 1612 after 267 years as owners. Rothiemay House was destroyed by fire and demolished in 1959.

High Street, Rothiemay. In 1630 the owner of Rothiemay, William Gordon, was burned to death in a fire at Frendraught House, Forgue, along with others including Viscount Melgum, a son of the Marquis of Huntly. The fire was something of a mystery, and investigations failed to find out exactly how it had started and – if it was deliberate – what the motive was. It is most likely that it was accidental, but nevertheless one man was executed for the crime and some servants were tortured in an attempt to obtain information. In 1741 the lands at Rothiemay were purchased by William Duff, Lord Braco (later first Earl Fife), and in 1751 the family obtained permission to move the church and churchyard in order to improve the view from Rothiemay House. The Duffs sold the estate in 1890 to Lieut-Col J. Foster Forbes.

George Pirrie & Son, Rothiemay.

The astronomer James Ferguson was born at Core of Mayen, Rothiemay, on 25 April 1710. Soon afterwards his family moved to the Forgieside district near Keith. Ferguson's formal education consisted of only three months at school in Keith under John Skinner. At the age of nine he went to work in the fields as a herd-boy, and at fourteen he was employed as a farm labourer by James Glashan at Ardneedlie (afterwards incorporated into Braehead). He showed a great interest in mechanical things, and one winter made a clock. After seeing a watch for the first time he made one himself within a month using wooden wheels and a whalebone spring. A turning point came when he showed some of his clocks to Sir James Dunbar of Durn, Portsoy. Dunbar employed him to clean clocks, and Lady Dipple gave him work as an artist and provided him with two years free lodging in Edinburgh, where he worked as an artist and studied anatomy and surgery.

High Street, Rothiemay. James Ferguson was fascinated by the stars, and in order to study them and their movements would lie down in a field at night, wrapped up in a blanket, with a candle at his side. He would hold a piece of string with beads on it in front of him to follow their movements, transferring the information he gathered to the map at his side. In 1743 he went to London where he remained for thirty-three years, lecturing, writing, compiling astronomical and other tables and constructing machines such as orreries (clockwork models of the planetary system), sundials, clocks and pumps. He appeared before King George III at Kew several times to demonstrate and explain his various inventions, and in 1762 the king granted him a pension of £50 a year. In 1763 he was elected a Fellow of the Royal Society. His publications included *Astronomy Explained Upon Sir Isaac Newton's Principles* (1765) and *Lectures on Mechanics, Hydrostatics, Pneumatics and Optics* (1760).

The earliest recorded teacher at Rothiemay was William Abernethie, a graduate of Marischal College, Aberdeen, who was appointed in 1612. Forty years later James Richardson was in charge of the school, but was dismissed for assaulting the minister's wife and her maids. Apparently, he had a grievance about his pay, and went to the minister's house one evening at 11 o'clock to try and resolve it. The minister wasn't there at the time, and after being asked to leave, Richardson slapped his wife around the ears with his gloves. When a female servant arrived on the scene he knocked her to the ground, injuring her face. Richardson's character and habits are vividly described as being 'scandalous by drinking and squabbling with soldiers, playing at dice to the loss of all his money, nay even his shirt' (Barclay, p257).

Grange Station. The Huntly to Keith line opened in 1856 and on 30 July 1859 a new line was opened from Grange to Banff & Portsoy. To allow trains from this new line to run to Aberdeen without returning to Grange (where they would have had to turn around), a short stretch of track was built to Cairnie Junction, half a mile east of Grange Station. In April 1895 Mrs Stewart, aged 66, of Garrowood, was returning from the merchant's shop at Grange Station when she was run over by a train. She was decapitated, both her legs were cut off, and her body was carried 60 yards along the line. In an accident in 1900 the guard from an Elgin to Grange train was killed at Grange by a workmen's train from Rothiemay which did not stop at the station.

Nethermills, Grange. In January 1915 the mill at Nethermills was completely destroyed by fire, but by October the same year it had been rebuilt and fitted with modern equipment. There was a new kiln for drying the grain, elevators for moving it, sieves for dressing it and bins for storage. The mill continued to be driven by water from the Isla. In the sixteenth century, when Grange was still joined to Keith parish, it was owned by the Abbey of Kinloss. The monks had a residence at Grange called the Tower of Strathisla, and farmed the area round about it. Abbot Crystall, who died at the Tower of Strathisla in 1535, had erected two mills in the area, one at Nethermills, the other at Newmill (now Old Newmill). The monastery at Kinloss, to which the Grange monks were attached, was founded in 1150 by King David I when he sent a colony of Cistercian monks from Melrose. They were known as the White Monks because of their dress, and maintained a strict silence, except during the time allowed for religious worship.